Security: Integrated Guarding

Security: Integrated Guarding

The 21st Century Residential and Commercial Real Estate Security Handbook

Steve Muntean

The author assumes total responsibility for meeting the requirements set by the United States copyright law for the inclusion of nay materials that are not the author's creation or in the public domain.

© Copyright 2017 Steve Muntean

All rights reserved

ISBN-13: 9781979972635
ISBN-10: 197997263X

Forward

In this handbook, you will learn about the evolution of security guard services and how to effectively protect real estate assets well into the 21st century. This is the future of security.

Technological advancement into the 21st century is evolving within the security service industry by transitioning from security guards to video monitoring-based integrated guarding solutions. Integrated guarding is shaping the future of how security professionals deploy protective services and protect assets.

This handbook explores the security guard services industry, video monitoring services, integrated guarding, and its effects on multi-family housing. Security guard services companies and venture capital firms are investing in integrated guarding due to the significant consumer and shareholder returns by leveraging technology, while reducing operating expenses. As new threats continue to emerge, security services, particularly integrated guarding, will have critical role in protecting the safety and security of our most valuable assets.

-- Steve Muntean

Contents

Section

Introduction · ix

Chapter 1 Trends: The Security Guard Industry · · · · · · · · · · · · · · · · · · · 1
Chapter 2 Trends: The Video Surveillance Industry· · · · · · · · · · · · · · · · 5
Chapter 3 United States Security Guard Industry Analysis · · · · · · · · · · 9
Chapter 4 United States Camera and Alarm Monitoring Industry
Analysis· ·13
Chapter 5 Trends: Integrated Guarding· ·16
Chapter 6 Integrated Guarding Affect, Case Study on
Multi-Family Real Estate· 20
Chapter 7 Conclusion ·24

References ·33

Introduction

As technology continues to emerge, many services are either being upgraded or replaced by systems that improve efficiencies and reduce costs. Innovation has changed the competitive landscape for businesses and the customers they service across the world. The technological shift is rapidly advancing and particularly relevant for human capital businesses operating in high risk and low margin environments.

The security services industry is one of the oldest employment sources in the world, having biblical references in the Old Testament and becoming a popular profession in the 1st century AD, operating worldwide and in a competitive business environment. Although thousands of years have passed, the essence of security guard services has relatively remained unchanged, until now.

Technological advancements have become a global phenomenon, age-old industries, such as security services have an opportunity to evolve. Evolution leveraged by changing market conditions can create an opportunity or significant challenges for industry stakeholders. When alternatives are available that produce affective results for a fraction of the cost, disruption occurs. Even an industry so historic, the security services sector will need to embrace technology, specifically the evolution of video surveillance to drive sustainability and maintain enterprise value.

As new threats continue to emerge the security services sector plays a critical role in protecting the safety and security of our nation. Most of the private security sector operates in a for-profit capacity and is often the front line of defense for our nation's well being. A significant portion of our nation's security personnel are responsible for protecting critical infrastructure including healthcare, energy, communications, transportation, commercial facilities, and financial services. The businesses employing these individuals offer a variety of services including unarmed, armed, dedicated, or patrol services.

The security services sector has grown significantly over the last decade and currently outnumbers the amount of sworn law enforcement officers in the United States.

Law enforcement agencies in the United States employ more than 760,000 sworn officers across 18,000 federal, state, and local departments (Storm, 2010). The number of outsourced security officers totaled nearly 800,000 employees; employed by roughly 8,000 contract security companies (Perry, 2015). The total employment data between law enforcement and security personnel, share a staggering similarity, the total between the two equal more than 1.56 million people tasked to protect our homeland.

This handbook is designed as a quick reference to explore how 21st century technological advancements are evolving the security services industry by transitioning from security guards to video monitoring-based integrated guarding solutions. The information is organized methodologically to present a diverse background providing multiple layers of industry specific information. The handbook explores data in the security guard services industry, video monitoring services, integrated guarding, and its effects on multi-family housing.

This handbook is focused on connecting resources to evaluate a growing problem in the security guard services industry. It is organized and designed to deliver information how technological advancements are changing the security services industry by transitioning from security guards to video monitoring based integrated guarding solutions. The chapters will provide an understanding of the security guard services industry, video surveillance industry, and the integrated guarding approach. The goal will help you understand an integrated case study within the commercial real-estate multi-family housing sector.

Chapter 1

Trends: The Security Guard Industry

The 2010 study, The Private Security Industry: A Review of the Definitions, Available Data Sources, and Paths Moving Forward form the National Criminal Justice Reference Service helps narrow the worldwide security viewpoint to the role security guard companies have in the United States (Storm, 2010). The information presented in the study outlines historical reference points and current state of the industry. This report uses factual data from Census Business Surveys, Bureau of Labor Statistics, and the Congressional Research Service. The study helps set the stage using statistical data to understand the industries scope and challenges.

G4S is the world's largest provider of security guard services. Since G4S is a publically traded company reviewing their 2015 Annual Report provides insight into the businesses performance, strategic initiatives, and financial health. The second largest provider of security guard services in the world is Securitas. Securitas is headquartered in Stockholm, Sweden and their 2015 Annual Report is also available for review. Their Annual Report provides significant insight into profit and loss statements, business trends, and future industry forecasts. Understanding the business operations for G4S and Securitas provide valuable insights into the security industry. Reviewing the two annual reports offer comparisons and differentiators on how each organization views the security guard services sector. Furthermore, these are the only two security guard companies that provide public access to mission critical business information.

The security guard industry is very fragmented where three companies represent over 44 percent of the United States domestic market share leaving the remaining 56 percent to be divided by more than 8,000 security guard services providers. It is estimated by Robert H. Perry and Associates, 7,000 of the 8,000 security guard services providers are between $0 to $5 million in annual revenue. This section will compare businesses performance, strategic initiatives, and financial health for G4S and Securitas.

The security guard services sector, one of the oldest industries in the world, experiences growth organically or through mergers and acquisitions. Robert H. Perry and Associates is the leading United States contract security expert in mergers and acquisitions. Mr. Perry publishes an annual report that reviews the market, margins, mergers, and multiples. The average organic growth of the three security guard service industry leaders is roughly 5 percent; the average growth for the remaining 99 percent of companies is 4 percent. Information outlined in the white paper report show the industry is trending away from standard guard services and towards integrated guarding with video monitoring leading the path. Interestingly enough, the integrated guarding services between G4S and Securitas AB have increased more than 25 percent per year.

The service offerings in the security guard services industry vary depending on location and vertical markets. The article, The Private Security Industry: A Review of the Definitions, Available Data Sources, and Paths Moving Forward helps frame the domestic security guard service industries specific target markets. Furthermore, the study provides valuable governmental census data on the current industry and trends impacting the nation's security. The largest sector spending, as a percentage of revenue, is education, including Colleges, Universities, and K-12. The second largest sector spending for security services is Casinos, Hospitality, Arenas, and Entertainment. It is important to highlight, the average spend for security services per employee in the Energy Utilities, Power, Gas, Nuclear, and Water sector has the highest expense at $31,504. The higher education average spend for security services per employee is $1,385, this represents a significant difference between critical utility infrastructure and educational security expenditures.

The security guard services industry is human capital intensive, the U.S. Department of Labor, Bureau of Labor Statistics (BLS) provides occupational employment and wages for Security Guards. The definition of Security Guards per the BLS is to guard, patrol, or monitor premises to prevent theft, violence, or infractions of rules. The reference points in the survey provide context, which is helpful in understanding the competitive nature of the industry.

Customers vary widely in the security guard services industry. The 2015 G4S Annual Report provides insight into their target markets and customer base. In this report, G4S claims to have a targeted growth rate between 4 to 6 percent with 90 percent or more of annual customer and contract retention. The G4S integrated guarding platform accounted for 8 percent of the group's total annual revenue. This annual report also provides information on the type of services offered specifically to each customer. The core G4S services include security consulting, monitoring and response, facilities management services, and manned and mobile security services. While G4S is the largest security provider in the world this data helps put into context the industries served by other security providers.

Over the last four years significant regulatory challenges have impacted the security guard industry. During the 2014 American Society for Industrial Security (ASIS) conference an educational session by presented by Eddie Sorrells outlined the impact of Obamacare on guard services providers. The session from Sorrells highlighted how the Affordable Care Act (ACA) has significant negative impacts on the contract security industry. Due to the industries intensive human capital business model and low wages, security companies typically have low profit margins and require volume to become profitable. The costs and/or fines associated with the ACA have increased the barrier to entry and cut profit margins for small to midsize contract security providers.

In addition to the ACA, another challenge the security guard services industry has is surrounding liability issues. Tory Brownyard, president of The Brownyard Group, outlines this liability concern in an article: How Large Jury Settlements Affect Enterprise Security. The contract security industry has a significant amount of liability due to the life and safety nature of industry.

General Liability insurance has become a necessity for anyone operating in this industry. Several large jury settlements, such as a $55 million verdict was awarded to a teenager shot by a gang member at an apartment complex, after a security officer failed to break up a gang party. The jury contended the officer did not warn the residents of danger by allowing the party to continue. Due to jury awards like this, insurance premiums associated with security services have become increasingly expensive and at times not available for security providers.

The U.S. government does not regulate the domestic security guard services industry. Each state has specific licensing regulations for companies and employees operating in a security capacity. Some states have more stringent regulatory control than others, due to the high-profile nature of armed security services, government regulation is an important role in keeping the public safe and ensuring companies are operating within judiciary guidelines. The Florida Department of Agriculture and Consumer Services is the state government agency responsible for regulating security services in the state of Florida. They have one of most compressive regulatory and licensing programs in the nation dividing company licenses into three agency categories: Class A, Private Investigative License; Class B, Security Agency License; and Class R, Recovery Agent License. The individual security officer has two types of licensing, Class D for Security Guard license and Class G for Armed Security Guard license. Each security guard employed must have a Florida D unarmed license and complete a mandated 40-hour course to perform services. Today, The Florida Department of Agriculture and Consumer Services has more than 80,000 D Licenses throughout the state of Florida. The Class G Armed Security Guard License mandates a 28-hour course must be completed with annual firearm re-qualifications, currently the state of Florida has more than 20,000 G licenses issued (DACS, 2017). The Georgia Secretary of State, Board of Private Security and Detectives regulate security guard and private detective services in the state of Georgia. Currently, Georgia has over 28,000 unarmed security guards and does not require state licensing to perform services (BLS, 2017). It is important to highlight the regulatory differences between these neighboring states since labor-licensing demographics impact the deployment of specific security services. This type of licensing differentiation is consistent nationwide and can cause operational concerns when provisioning security services across state boundaries.

Chapter 2

Trends: The Video Surveillance Industry

The video surveillance industry is one of the fastest growing segments within the security industry. Markets and Markets, the largest worldwide market research reporting firm, estimates the video surveillance market will be worth $71.28 billion by 2022 at an estimated Compound Annual Growth Rate of 16.56 percent. This significant growth rate means two things, first the demand for video surveillance is increasing and the effectiveness from technological advancements is improving. This study helps breakdown the industries revenue streams by the System (Analog, IP), Component (Camera, Monitor, Server, Storage Device, Software), Service (VSaaS, Maintenance), Application (Infrastructure, Commercial, Institutional, Defense, residential), and Geography. The largest purchaser segment expected to adopt video surveillance hardware technology over the next 5 years is the commercial sector, specifically the commercial real estate industry.

Barnes Associates is the leading merger and acquisition expert in the U.S. Video Surveillance and Alarm industry. The Annual Barnes Buchanan Conference in Palm Beach, FL, discusses past performance and industry trends. Michael Barnes, Founding Partner of Barnes Associates reported the security alarm industries total revenues reached $55 billion, a 6 percent growth rate in 2016, following a 5 percent growth in 2015. In 2016, $312 million of recurring monthly revenue (RMR) traded at an average multiple of 45-times

RMR. In 2015, $77 million of RMR traded at the same average multiple of 45 times (SDM, 2017).

Video surveillance labor forces vary significantly from the security guard services industry. The U.S. Department of Labor, Bureau of Labor Statistics (BLS) provides occupational employment and wages for video surveillance installers combined with alarm and fire alarm system installers. By definition, security and fire alarm system installers are similar to video surveillance installers since they install, program, maintain, and repair security and fire alarm wiring and equipment. As of May 2015, the average wage rates for this profession are significantly higher than the security guard services industry ranging from $13.13 to $30.94 per hour.

The video surveillance industry, particularly camera hardware and real-time monitoring, has come under significant scrutiny due to liability, private VS public civil liberties, and government oversight. The Constitution Project released a comprehensive study, *Guidelines for Public Video Surveillance*, focused on protecting communities and preserving civil liberties. The Constitution Project highlights technological and social advancements having created a powerful network of video systems capable of high resolution monitoring, motion detection, infrared vision, and biometric identification. This enhanced technology is capable of never before seen public automated tracking, archiving, and identifying suspect behavior having citizens concerned their civil rights are being infringed. Many local municipalities deploying these enhanced camera networks are using federal anti-terrorism grants to build infrastructure.

In addition to the civil right infringements, Arthur J. Gallagher Risk Management Services, issued a White Paper highlighting several key liability concerns with video surveillance for public sector clients. His first concern is Tort law requires the property owner to take reasonable responsibility to ensure the safety of those persons who are on the property legally. Although, the property owner cannot predict the future they do have a reasonable right to foreseeability about potential security issues they were privileged to and/or had knowledge about that a normal person would not typically have knowledge of.

Security: Integrated Guarding

21st Century Security, The Intergraded Guarding Approach

The security guard services industry has a unique opportunity to capitalize on new technology integrated with a familiar business model to change the landscape of 21st century security. Security professionals look for alternative effective solutions that reduce operating expenses and increase results. This trend is supported by significant research outlining the benefits of video surveillance cameras, specifically when they are monitored in real-time and have law enforcement or security response.

Over the last few years the contract security industry has experienced significant growth in acquisitions for real-time video monitoring, the U.S. alarm monitoring and service revenue is now at $25 billion, up 8 percent in 2016. Moreover, the acquirers purchasing these real-time video monitoring firms are security guard services companies whose primary business model is focused on physical security guards. The combination of real-time video monitoring and security guard services represent a new term called Integrated Guarding.

Integrated Guarding refers to real-time video monitoring services combined with security patrol and/or law enforcement response to events witness by virtual monitoring operators. The competitive landscape in the integrated guarding industry encompasses small, medium, and large companies. G4S represents the largest integrated guarding company, their security systems and technology division, represents more than 8 percent of G4S total revenue. Thrive Monitoring is a midsized integrated guarding company acquired in 2013 by privately held Allied Universal, the United States third largest security guard services company. WideEye Surveillance is a venture capital backed real-time monitoring company providing third-party security guard companies the ability to offer video monitoring without the large capital expenditures of having a central monitoring station.

Integrated guarding is the leading innovative service within the security sector. This emerging technology has not only been driving change in the security guard services industry it has been shaping central stations within the video surveillance and monitoring sector. An article titled, *The Crime Rate Drops, and a City Credits Its Embrace of Surveillance Technology* highlight the success of integrated guarding. This report summarizes the integration of

CCTV and law enforcement patrol tactics in East Orange, N.J. The article explains the use of real-time CCTV and electronic listening devices across the city of 70,000. The system was deployed from 2003 to 2006, during this time murders declined by nearly two-thirds and robberies were cut by half.

A similar integrated guarding approach was implemented at the University of Southern California. In 2007, the university began installing cameras and providing real-time monitoring focusing on license plate recognition in neighborhoods around the campus. The Chief of Public Safety, Carey Drayton, quotes "video patrol differs from CCTV because everybody else puts cameras up and hopes to catch something. What we're doing is using the force multiplier of putting people to respond and technology that allows one person sitting at a console to be able to video patrol an area around the location of camera." During 2003 to 2007 this technology was cutting edge and expensive allowing only government agencies or law enforcement agencies the ability to use them. Now, 10 years later the private sector can deploy this integrated technology and achieve similar results for a fraction of the cost.

Chapter 3

United States Security Guard Industry Analysis

The role of security throughout the United States has experienced significant growth over the last decade. Industry acquisitions have led the majority of growth initiatives however technology enhancements have leveled the market and valuations multipliers have increased. The qualitative data analyzed presents valuable insight into the security guard services, video monitoring, and integrated guarding sector.

The security guard services industry is highly fragmented with three companies owning more than 44 percent of a $23 billion dollar per year market.

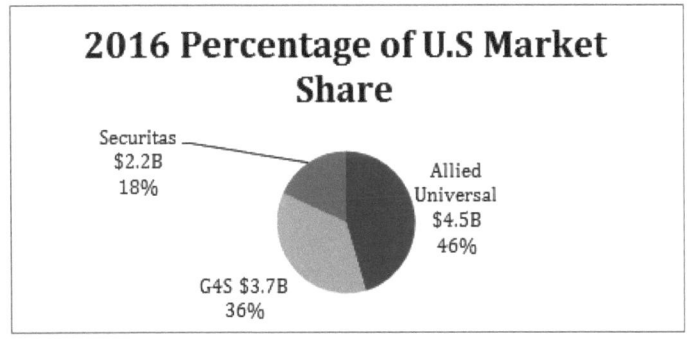

Figure 1.1 Three Security Guard Services Industry Leaders 2016
Source: Robert H. Perry and Associates, July 2016 White Paper on the United States Contract Security Guard Industry.

The three industry leaders have a blended organic growth rate of 5 percent. The EBITDA margins vary depending on scale and revenue mix, not all revenue in the security guard services is created equal.

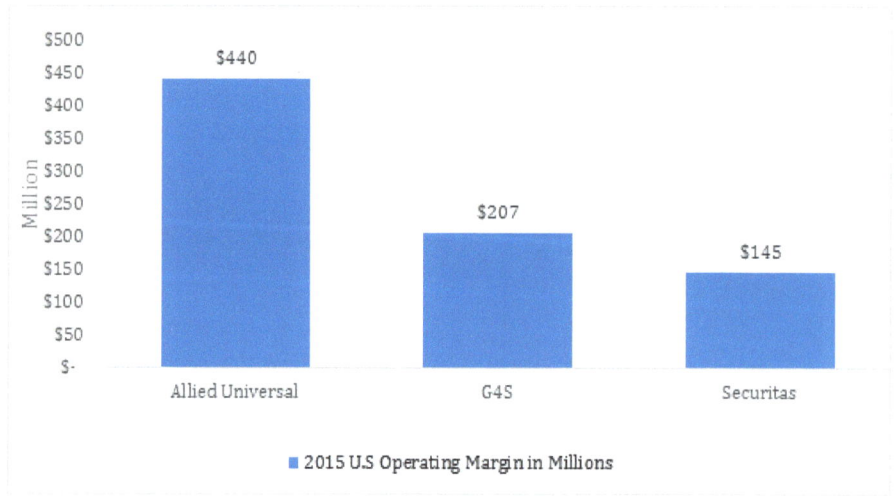

Figure 1.2 United States Revenue and Operating Margin from Allied Universal, G4S, and Securitas (2015).
Source: Robert H. Perry and Associates, July 2016 White Paper on the U.S. Contract Security Guard Industry.

In 2016, it is estimated 8,000 security guard companies perform contract services within the United States equaling $23 billion in combined revenue. Less than 96 percent of companies are likely less than $5,000,000 in annual revenue.

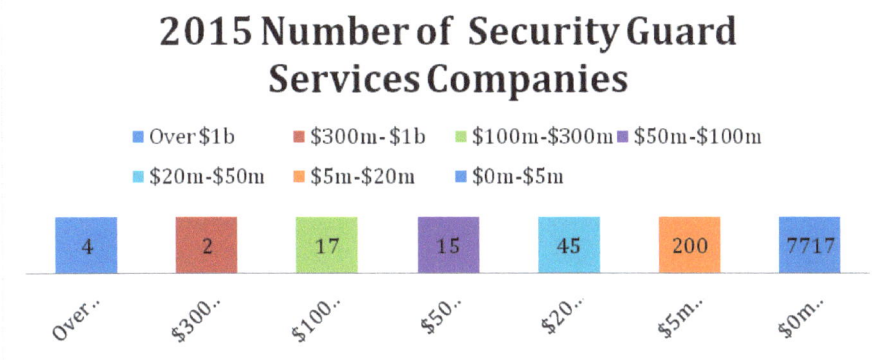

Figure 1.3 Size of the Industry and Number of Companies
Source: Robert H. Perry and Associates, July 2016 White Paper on the United States Contract Security Guard Industry.

In the United States, security companies employ more than 800,000 security personnel. Law enforcement agencies in the United States employ more than 760,000 sworn officers across 18,000 federal, state, and local departments (Storm, 2010). In 2016 Allied Universal, Securitas, and G4S employed more than 312,000 contract security personnel. Allied Universal employed 150,000, Securitas employed 108,000, and G4S employed 54,000. The security guard average hourly wage rate in the United States is $11.84 per hour.

Percentile	10%	25%	50% (Median)	75%	90%
Hourly Wage	$8.82	$9.80	$11.84	$15.87	$21.64
Annual Wage (2)	$18,350	$20,370	$24,630	$33,000	$45,010

Figure 1.4 2015 Wage Statistics for 33-9032 Security Guards
Source: The United States Department of Labor, Bureau of Labor Statistics, 2015 Wage Statistics for 33-9032 Security Guards

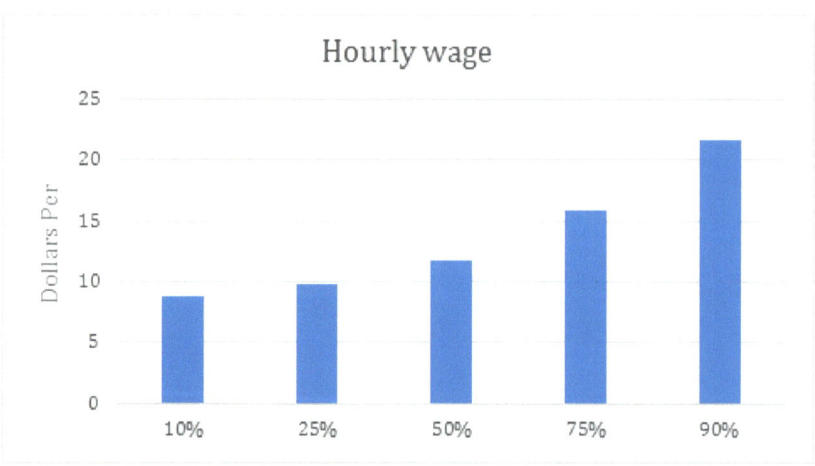

Figure 1.5 2015 Wage Chart 33-9032 Security Guards
Source: The United States Department of Labor, Bureau of Labor Statistics, 2015 Wage Statistics for 33-9032 Security Guards

It is important to understand the distribution of how security budgets are allocated per industry sector. Industries with larger security budgets employ more security personnel. The industries spending the most on security services become the largest target customer for security service industries.

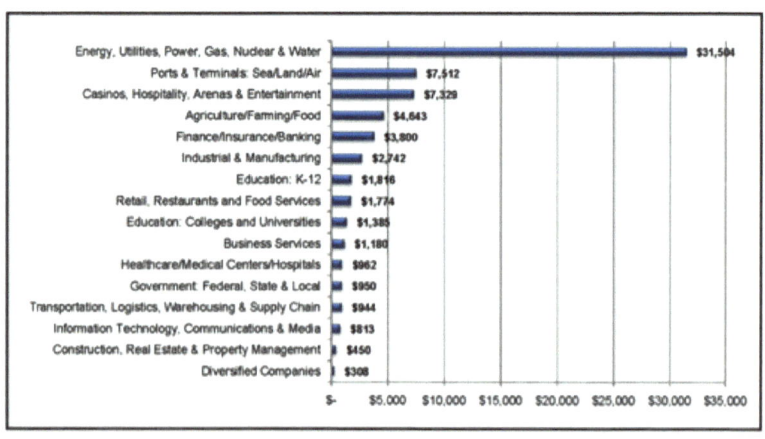

Figure 1.6: 2009 Largest Security Contracts by Industry
Source: Security Magazine (McCourt, 2009)

Chapter 4

United States Camera and Alarm Monitoring Industry Analysis

Markets and Markets, the largest market research reporting firm worldwide, estimates the video surveillance market will be worth $71.28 billion by 2022 at an estimated Compound Annual Growth Rate of 16.56 percent.

Barnes Associates, the leading U.S. Video Surveillance Alarm security expert in mergers and acquisitions held the 22nd Annual Barnes Buchanan Conference this February in Palm Beach, FL, discussing past performance and industry trends. Michael Barnes, Founding Partner of Barnes Associates outlined the security alarm industries total revenues reached $55 billion, a 6 percent growth rate in 2016, following a 5 percent growth in 2015.

In total 2016, $312 million of recurring monthly revenue (RMR) traded at an average multiple of 45-time RMR. In 2015, $77 million of RMR traded at the same average multiple of 45 times (SDM, 2017). It is important to note the 2016 transaction increase from $77 million to $312 million included $60 million of RMR from the ADT transaction.

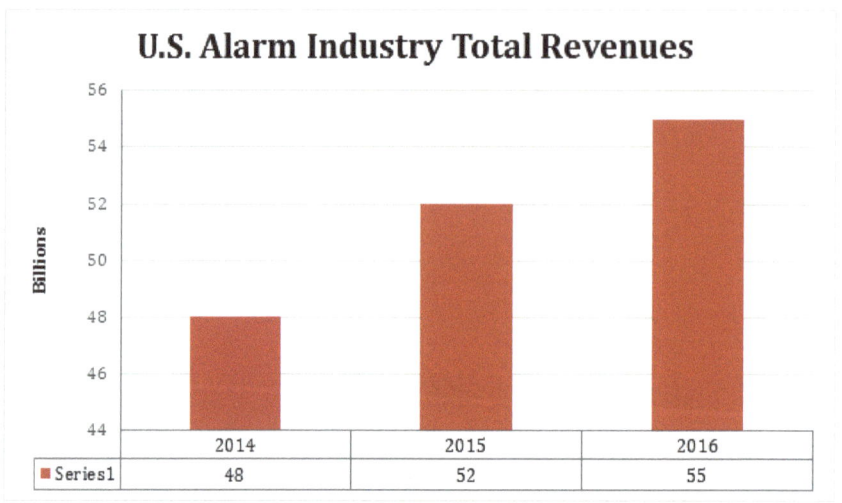

Figure 2.1 2014-2016 U.S. Alarm Industry Total Revenue
Source: 2017 Barnes Buchanan Conference

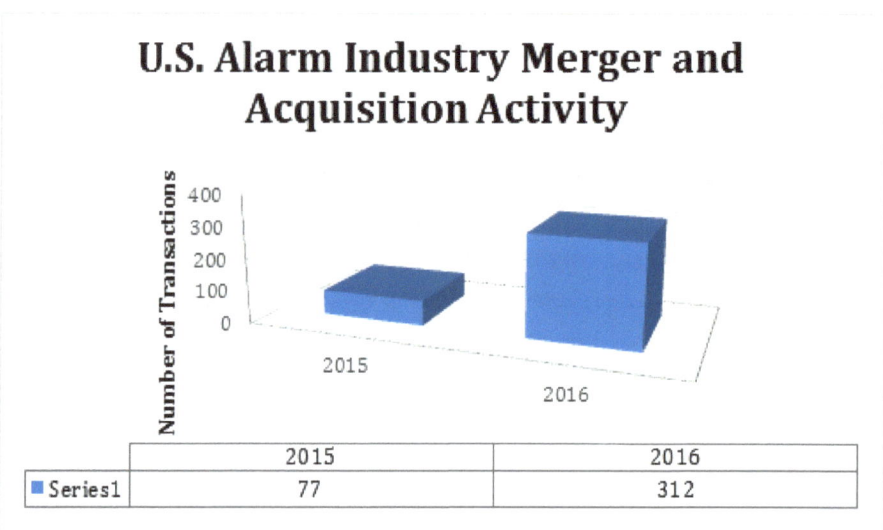

Figure 2.2 2015-2016 U.S. Alarm Industry Merger and Acquisition
Source: SDM, Security Distribution and Marketing

Security: Integrated Guarding

The alarm industry consists of two revenue streams, one from hardware/installation revenue and the other from alarm monitoring revenue. From the $52 billion revenues in 2016, $25 billion was generated from alarm and monitoring services. The remaining $27 billion was generated from installation and hardware revenue. Similar to the security guard services sector the alarm industry is highly fragmented with two large industry leaders, Tyco International and ADT Corporation.

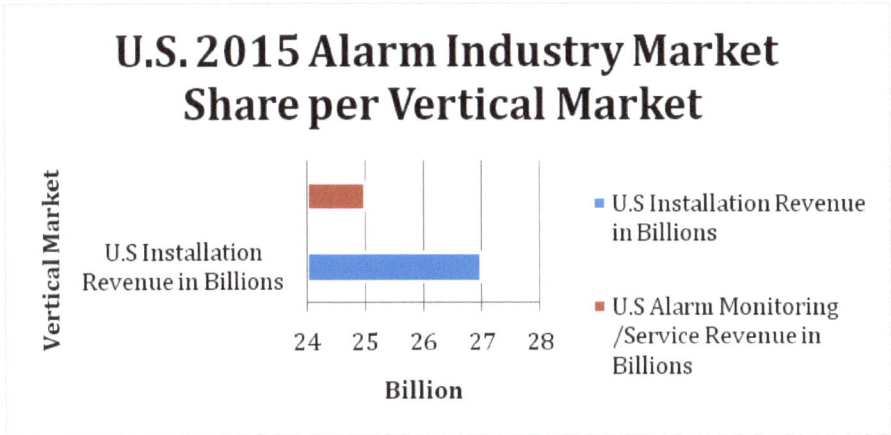

Figure 2.3 2015 Alarm Industry Market Share by Revenue Source
Source: Robert H. Perry and Associates, July 2016 White Paper on the United States Contract Security Guard Industry.

Chapter 5

Trends: Integrated Guarding

Since 2013, Integrated Guarding services have become a leading trend in the security guard and security alarm industry. The three security guard industry leaders, Allied Universal, G4S, and Securitas have recently acquired Integrated Guarding divisions to offer commercial security monitoring services similar to Tyco International and ADT however they maintain a close relationship with their commercial customers who require security guard services.

G4S Technology, a division of the United States third largest security services company G4S, launched in 2013 to focus on developing a call center and hosted video monitoring center. In December 2016, G4S purchased a Canadian video and security systems company, i-Vision. Securitas Integrated Guarding purchased a 24% equity position in Iverify during 2014. Shortly thereafter in February 2016 Securitas also purchased Diebold as a strategic middle market partner who provided electronic security, their revenue at the time of acquisition were $330 million. In 2013, Allied Universal purchased Thrive Intelligence who provides monitoring and video camera hardware. WideEye Surveillance received Venture Capital Funding in March 2014 from Unit Economic Investors who is focused on early stage investments within the security industry.

Security: Integrated Guarding

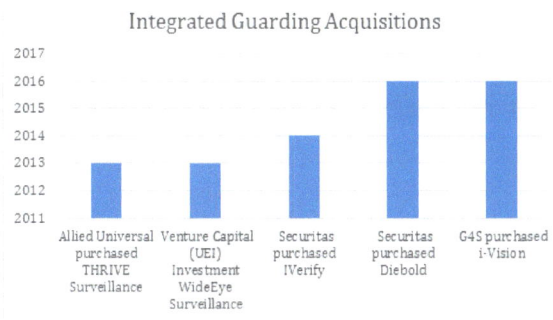

Figure 3.1 2013-2016 Integrated Guarding Mergers and Acquisitions

The recent Intergraded Guarding acquisition and investment strategy in the security services sector from 2013 to 2017 represents a shift how leveraging technology improves security measures. One of the early public sector case studies highlighting the success of Integrated Guarding was implemented in East Orange, N.J. The city integrated real-time video monitoring and electronic listening devices across the city of 70,000. The system was deployed in 2003 to 2006, during this time murders declined by nearly two-thirds and robberies were cut by half (Jones, 2007).

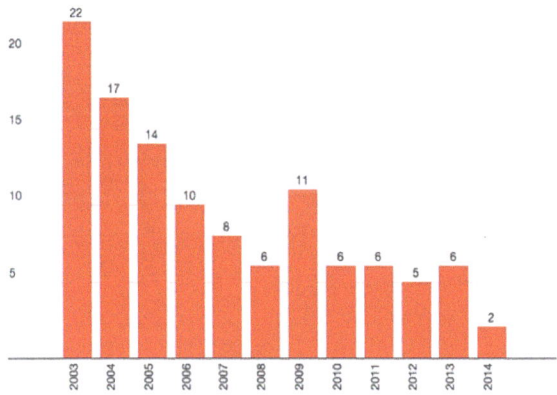

Figure 3.2 Murder Rate Reduction in Orange City from 2003-2014
Source: The New York Times, Crime Rate Drops, and a City Credits Its Embrace of Surveillance Technology.

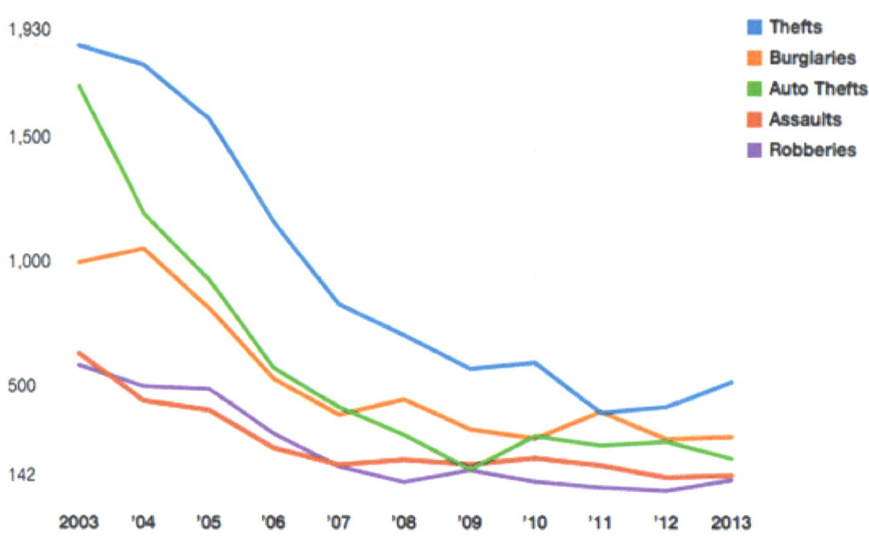

Figure 3.3 Crime Reduction Type in Orange City form 2003-2013
Source: The New York Times, Crime Rate Drops, and a City Credits Its Embrace of Surveillance Technology.

The University of Southern California's (USC) Department of Public Safety is responsible for protecting a 6-square-mile area that includes the campus, residential, and commercial areas. The innovative approach to Integrated Guarding includes a combination of real-time camera monitoring, security patrol officers, police officers, and security ambassadors. With this combination USC has reduced Clery Act-reported crimes by more than 50 percent from 2006 to 2012. Furthermore, after installing dome cameras on light poles in neighborhoods bordering USC, the number of robberies reduced from 22 to zero in a six-month period in 2006.

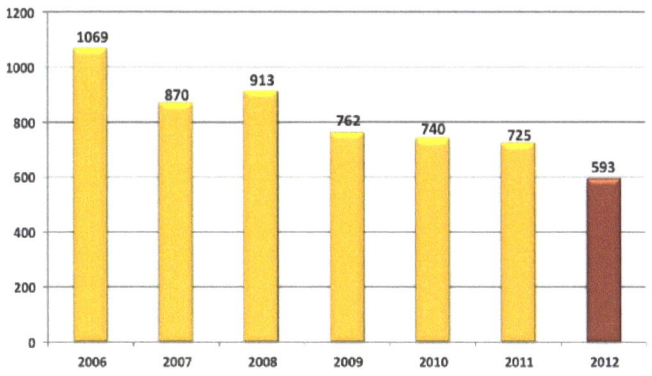

Figure 3.4 USC Crime Reduction from 2006-2012
Source: Campus Safety Magazine – USC Campus Security

The use of real time video monitoring has significantly served as a force multiplier for private and public sector personnel. When video monitoring operators identify criminal and suspicious behavior they can capture the act in real time then dispatch a responding agency. There is an estimated 30 million surveillance cameras throughout the United States recording more than 4 billion hours of footage per week. The total number of law enforcement and security professionals totals a little over 1.5 million, with their being 30 million active surveillance cameras, surveillance cameras outnumber physical staff by 20:1.

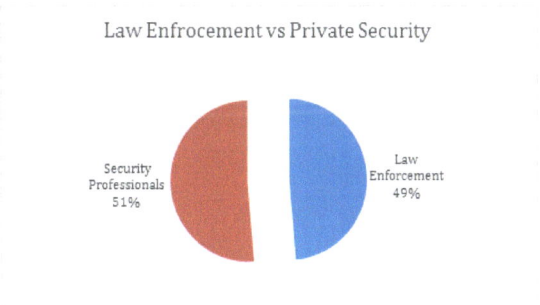

Figure 3.5: 2016 Law Enforcement and Private Security Employees
Source: The Private Security Industry: A Review of the Definitions, Available Data Sources, and Paths Moving Forward

Chapter 6

Integrated Guarding Affect, Case Study on Multi-Family Real Estate

The security guard services sector has many vertical markets where security services are deployed. The Construction, Real Estate, and Property Management sector represented the fourth-largest employment group for security guard services in the nation (Storm, 2010). Real Estate, particularly multi-family housing is one of the fastest growing industries in the country. A significant population in United States relies on multi-family housing for affordable and safe living options.

Over the last decade the amount of renter-occupied from owner-occupied housing options has increased significantly. In 2016, more than 37 percent of households in the United States were renter-occupied and responsible for housing more than 111,118,925 people (NMCH, 2016). The National Multifamily Housing Counsel estimates large cities such as New York, Los Angeles, Chicago, and San Francisco account for more than 42 percent of renter-occupied households. Renter-occupied housing is becoming an expanding option for all demographics. It offers many distinct advantages and disadvantages, the largest advantage is a desirable location and reduced cost of living while a significant disadvantage is the increased criminal activity due to the typical metropolitan area and associated criminal activity.

The Federal Bureau of Investigation (FBI) completes a Semi-annual Uniform Crime Report having a particular emphasis on violent crime. Based on an FBI report, violent crimes increased in 2016, in all large metropolitan counties. In cities with populations more than 1 million, violent crimes rose 9.7 percent, in cities with populations from 500,000 to 999,999 violent crime increased 5.2 percent, and in cities with 250,000 to 499,999 inhabitants violent crime was up 4.3 percent (FBI, 2017). In 2016 the overall violent crime increased from 2015, 6.3 percent of that increase was in metropolitan counties and 1.6 percent was in non-metropolitan counties.

The multi-family housing industry has many security challenges especially in large metropolitan cities. Over the last decade, the increase in violent crime and property crime nationwide has impacted multi-family owners, their residents, and the security industry. The increase in criminal activity has promoted the litigious environment to undertake legal claims against multifamily owners and security companies often awarding multi-million dollar liability claims to residents and guests claiming negligence. The Federation of Defense and Corporate Counsel released a white paper titled, *Negligent Security, When is Crime your Problem* highlighting negligent security issues. The study outlined significant multi-family negligent case law over the last decade ranging from traditional housing to government subsidized housing. In the 2010 trial, *Gonzalez v. Parkchester South Condominium*, New York Supreme Court the plaintiff, Ms. Gonzales, was raped at gunpoint within the condominium complex. The New York Police Department (NYPD) has records indicating the complex had developed a pattern of increased crime and was notified by a NYPD detective they should increase security precautions (Ford, 2011). Since the defendant did not implement additional security measures the jury awarded the victim $975,000.

Traditionally security services for the multi-family industry have been focused on a dedicated security guard either providing access control or conducting foot patrols. This type of dedicated security service has now become obsolete and ineffective due technological enhancements. Recently, owners and security providers have developed a partnership focused on reducing crime to protect the investment asset and provide residents a secure environment. Security solutions specifically designed for multi-family housing have expanded, technology has improved and new security companies have entered the competitive landscape.

A research study titled, *The Effectiveness of an Electronic Security Management System in a Privately Owned Apartment Complex* discusses the advantages of video cameras in Peter Cooper Village located in New York City. The study finds video cameras are effective in preventing minor crimes or diverting them to distant areas (Greenberg, 2009). In addition, the effectiveness of video cameras must be tied to monitoring and have a response when needed to show the value of the camera hardware investment.

Case Study

A multi-family community with 450 units located near downtown Atlanta, GA, had significant felony criminal issues. In 2015, the community ownership decided to implement an integrated guarding approach by installing 44 cameras throughout the community and contracting a security guard services company to provide targeted vehicle patrols. During the inception of integrated guarding the community reported a decrease in crime, in 2014 the community had 66 reported violent crime incidents, 2015 has 28 incidents, and 2016 ended with 19 incidents.

Figure 4.3: 2014-2016 Atlanta, GA Apartment Community Crime Reduction
Source: The Spillers Group, John Spillers.

Security: Integrated Guarding

The integrated guarding approach has proven effective in both private and public sector environments. Security guard services companies and venture capital firms are investing in integrated guarding due to significant consumer and security company benefits. Integrated guarding will be shaping the future of how security professionals deploy services and protect assets.

Chapter 7

Conclusion

The purpose of this study explored how 21st century technological advancements are evolving the security service industry by transitioning from security guards to video monitoring based integrated guarding solutions. The methodology explored qualitative data in the security guard services industry, video monitoring services, integrated guarding, and its effects on multi-family housing. The qualitative research strategy tested relationships using secondary dates sources form the security guard service industry and video monitoring industry.

In 2015, the U.S. contract security guard industry generated more than $43 billion in revenue (Perry, 2015). As outlined is Chapter 4, the security guard industry is fragmented where G4S, Securitas, and Allied Universal own more than 40 percent of the market share totaling more than $12 billion in combined revenue. The growing ratio of contract security agencies compared to law enforcement agencies is 2:1. The security industry has a versatile and growing role in the overall safety and security of our nation.

Over the last decade innovation has provided the security guard industry the ability to evolve, and leverage technology to produce a safer environment. Furthermore, most growth derived in the contract security industry is a result of a share-shift contract strategy, minor service differentiators, or through mergers and acquisitions. In 2015, the United States contract security sector experienced a blended 4 percent growth rate, mostly through mergers and acquisitions. This slow growth rate combined with declining profit margins due to increased operating expenses is forcing the industry to re-evaluate long-term growth and sustainment strategies. The security services environment is responsible for life and safety, leaving little room for errors resulting from poor corporate governance or failed growth strategies.

Technological advancements throughout social and business frameworks have transformed industries over the last decade. The evolution of video surveillance has been one of these technological advancements, changing the security industry landscape. The combination of upgraded camera hardware, software analytics, and increased bandwidth has made video surveillance a reliable security force multiplier. Furthermore, the cost for video surveillance solutions has decreased as the competitive landscape has driven operating costs down while business efficiencies have improved.

The global video surveillance market generated an estimated $15.5 billion in revenue in 2015. While this is a fraction compared to the $43 billion in revenue security service sector, many experts forecast in 2020 the video surveillance market will reach $71.28 billion (Markets, 2016). This projection represents significant growth in the video surveillance sector, however, this forecast is comparable to many technological based industries that have replaced or replicated manual labor industries such as the security services sector.

Although the video surveillance and alarm industry is experiencing significant growth it is difficult to fully compare video surveillance cameras and their benefits to the security guard industry. The technological breakthroughs in security systems developed over the last few years have closed the gap from standard video surveillance and security guards to a more integrated approach. Integrated guarding combines video camera hardware, fiber optic bandwidth, virtual monitoring operators, and a security patrol response. This approach has gained momentum from security professionals across the world due to the increased effectiveness and reduced operating expenses.

Today, there are an estimated 30 million surveillance cameras deployed in the United States, shooting roughly 4 billion hours of footage per week

(Vlahos, 2009). Considering there at 1.5 million security and law enforcement professionals throughout the United States, surveillance cameras outnumber public safety professionals 20:1. Civilian video surveillance cameras do not possess human qualities since they are machines; this provides cameras many distinct competitive advantages over humans. Some of these characteristics include the ability to record 24/7/365 regardless of weather conditions and human sensory feelings such as being tired, sick, or unproductive. Furthermore, surveillance cameras record specific footage that is subject to minimal interpretation versus a human's recollection of an event can be distorted and inaccurate. A human's interpretations of an event can significantly vary depending on the individual's culture, experiences, and world perceptions to name a few.

The contract security guard industry relies heavily on human capital to run their businesses. Unfortunately, most security guard companies offer minimal compensation and benefit structures, due to historically low-margin structures. The security sectors competitive low margin nature can produce quality of service issues and infective results due to marginal operating restrictions. Over last four years, the security guard industry has experienced devastating impacts from governmental regulations from mandatory minimum wage increases, the Affordable Care Act, and Department of Labor Overtime Rulings. Furthermore, significant general liability and workers compensation insurance has increased to record levels due to an unprecedented amount of insurance claims against security companies, their employees, and the customers they service. Over the last four years the increase in regulation and additional insurance burdens has raised operating expenses more than 10 percent for most security guard companies while hourly revenue bill rates remain the same.

The security landscape with an emphasis on video surveillance and security guards is evolving to meet the expanding nature of threats. Countermeasures against man-made threats on private property is now becoming a necessity due to increased crime, liability concerns, and growing government regulations. Since most private commercial property is occupied for a profit thought Real Estate Investment Trusts (RITS) or similar ownership structures the

Security: Integrated Guarding

stakeholders must balance the risk vs. reward of security expenditures. Most commercial real estate owners have chosen surveillance cameras as their security countermeasures due to cost and reduced liability.

Traditionally, surveillance cameras have been used to review after the fact events by building historical timelines and suspect information for judiciary proceedings. While capturing information that leads to prosecution is helpful, it does not necessarily deter criminal activity. With new technology advancements, innovative tools have become available to convert surveillance cameras into proactive crime deterrence solutions. The previous thought process for many commercial real estate owners was to install security cameras, knowing it was not effective; however, meet the legal requirements set forth by insurance carriers and government subsidy regulators. This unfortunately has changed as new civil liability torts have evolved and criminal behavior is becoming more frequent with devastating results. Today, the traditional video surveillance solution is not enough to protect assets and security guards are often ineffective and cost prohibitive.

When security alternatives are available that can produce affective results for a fraction of the cost, industries evolve. Security guard companies are experiencing expanding regulation, increased operating expenses, and human capital management challenges. Video surveillance solutions have become more affordable and reliable than their predecessors several years ago, however, the cameras alone do not replicate nor replace a security guard. The combination of new technological advancements in video surveillance, especially in real-time video monitoring, will create a shift in security solutions leading the path for an integrated platform including camera hardware, real-time video surveillance, and security patrol.

As technology continues to emerge, many services are either being upgraded or replaced by more efficient services and cost reductions. This type of innovation has changed the competitive landscape for companies across the nation. For example, consider how Uber has disrupted the taxicab industry, what Amazon has done to brick and mortar retail stores, and how military drones are replacing fighter pilots. Innovation is being adopted in this industry at a rapid rate focused on reducing operating expenses and increasing results.

Investors, especially in the commercial and multi-family real estate sector are results orientated and price sensitive. When security alternatives are available that can produce affective results for a fraction of the cost industries are disrupted. The emergence of video surveillance, specifically integrated guarding, is disrupting the traditional security guard industry and the customers they serve due to increased effectiveness and cost reductions.

The integrated guarding approach has proven very effective at streamlining operations and reducing crime. In Orange City, N.J., when integrated guarding was deployed from 2003 to 2006, murders declined by nearly two-thirds and robberies were cut by half (Jones, 2007). The University of Southern California's (USC) Department of Public Safety implemented integrated guarding, by doing this they reduced Clery Act-reported crimes by more than 50 percent from 2006-2012 and number of robberies reduced from 22 to zero in a six-month period in 2006. Fortunately, law enforcement agencies typically have large operating budgets to support massive video monitoring integrations and strategic personnel deployments.

This integrated guarding approach has been deployed since 2003, however it took more than 10 years for security guard service companies, the first acquisition by Allied Universal for Thrive Monitoring was in 2013, to integrate this approach. One of the major restrictions for this was the technology was not scalable and was cost prohibitive. Many high-tech video systems were out-of-reach for most commercial applications and reserved for government deployments. Today, video systems are available for a fraction of the cost and can be used as a force multiplier for security guard service companies.

One of the largest security guard services and security alarm customer segments who leverage real-time video monitoring is Construction, Real Estate, and Property Management. These housing sectors represent the 4th largest employment sector for security guard services in the nation (Storm, 2010). Within these sectors, Multi-family housing represents a significant growth vertical considering more than 37 percent of households in the United States are renter-occupied and responsible for housing more than 111,118,925 people (NMCH, 2016). Large metropolitan cities represent more than 42 percent of renter-occupied households while violent crimes increased in all

Security: Integrated Guarding

large metropolitan counties. In 2016, cities with populations of more than 1 million, violent crimes rose 9.7 percent. When metropolitan cities experience a population density expansion and an increase in violent crime, community stakeholders must re-evaluate security alternatives.

Traditionally, security services for the multi-family industry have been focused on a variety of security solutions including security guards, video cameras, lighting, fencing, and access control. These are all helpful security solutions when defending a community however each has a capital expense and need to be maintained regularly to be effective. Over the last decade the most common multi-family security defense has become a dedicated security officer providing access control or conducting foot patrols. Due to shrinking margins in the security guard services industry, increasing violent crime, urbanization, and low labor participation rates a professional dedicated security officer in multi-family housing is not a sustainable option.

Integrated guarding has become a growing trend in the security guard services and security alarm industry. Integrated guarding combines real-time video monitoring and security, or law enforcement patrol response. Over the last four years, the three largest United States security guard services business invested in real-time monitoring companies to begin the integrated guarding evolution. Venture Capital firms have also invested in companies providing real-time monitoring to offering integrated guarding solutions.

The Integrated guarding approach is designed to leverage human capital expenses, by having video monitoring operators conduct virtual surveillance to mimic a dedicated security guard. When video monitoring operators notice something or someone suspicious they dispatch the appropriate security or law enforcement officer. Responding personnel have real-time information to where the suspicious activity is located and a description of the event or suspects. This process allows targeted oriented security similar to how Orange City, N.J., and the USC Department of Public Safety were able to reduce violent crime by 50 percent.

On average it takes a dedicated security guard 30 to 60 minutes to conduct a detailed patrol of a multi-family community. Video monitoring operators can conduct a minimum of 6 patrols at the same community during the same duration for a fraction of the cost. Another advantage of integrated guarding is the video monitoring hardware does not possess the human qualities that cause quality of service issues.

Figure 4.1 Video Monitoring can be 6 Time more Effective than a Security Patrol
Source: wideeyesurveillance.com

The financial benefit of migrating from a security guard towards integrated guarding can have a substantial savings. The average cost to hire a dedicated security guard in the United States is $20 per hour, whereas the average video monitoring patrol is $6. Based on an 8-hour shift, 7 days per week, 365 days per year the dedicated security guard costs $57,792 and the video monitoring patrol is $17,337 per year. This represents a $40,500 annual savings. In addition, the indirect benefits of video monitoring vs. a dedicated security guard will reduce liability insurance and increase resident retention. Integrated guarding has multiple benefits for security guard companies and multi-family consumers.

Security: Integrated Guarding

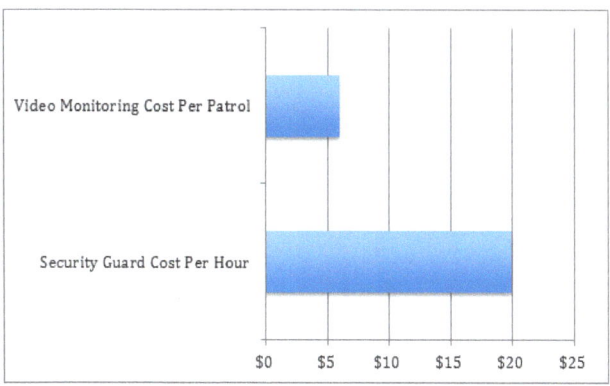

Figure 4.2 Video Monitoring can be 6 times more effective than a Security Patrol
Source: WideEye Surveillance, http://wideeyesurveillance.com/

Currently, there is a small fraction of the 8,000 security guard service companies providing integrated guarding (real-time video monitoring and physical security response). This technology-based innovation is disrupting the security services sector. Integrated guarding market penetration has been limited, thus far, for most security industry leaders due to many internal corporate challenges.

For security companies, the first integrated guarding adoption challenge is coming to terms with revenue reduction. Since Integrated guarding costs a fraction of the traditional dedicated guarding services, the shift to video monitoring from dedicated services reduces top line revenue. For example, a security guard company with a $350,000 annual dedicated guarding contract, when integrated guarding is introduced will reduce the annual contract value to $222,000, a $128,000 revenue loss. Although the gross profit margin can be more it is difficult for most executives to cannibalize their revenue by more than 35%. The second challenge is security guard companies operate as services business, real-time video monitoring involves significant technology deployments and a new business model shift many security operators have never deployed nor have the management team to implement. The third challenge is only a few security providers have the balance sheet to pioneer real-time monitoring and integrated guarding, less than 1% of the 8,000 contract security providers are executing integrated guarding platforms.

Although real-time monitoring is in its infancy stage, more technological advancements supporting integrated guarding are disrupting the security industry. Tomorrow's security guard may be paired with an autonomous robot, similar to the machines now available from Knightscope. Knightscope machines have traveled more than 100,000 miles and are making a significant impact on crime. This technology will provide real time access to detections allowing the deployment of mobile guards who will be able make smarter, faster and safer decisions. The deployment of Knightscope machines (K1, K3, K5, and K7) cost a fraction of the physical security guards they are replacing and can operate 24/7/365.

On-demand location based services applications will become another disrupter in the security industry in similar to the effect Uber and Lyft have on the taxi transportation industry. The market leader, Guardopolis, pairs customers requesting a security response with qualified security vendors and off-duty law enforcement personnel. Guardopolis's mobile application will end ineffective long-term contracts and minimum daily service hours with a system locating the nearest security provider, paying for services only when you need them, and matching a provider with your specific needs.

21st century technological advancements are disrupting the security industry. Security guard companies specifically servicing multi-family and commercial real-estate clients will need to evolve. Client expectations to generate shareholder returns and manage risk will drive integrated guarding to meet growing demands. Innovations in integrated guarding specifically real-time video monitoring, autonomous robots, and on-demand security applications will become the norm. The next decade will shift customer expectations and security business models toward integrated guarding; only the innovative will survive and produce effective security solutions.

References

2015 G4S Annual Report - Strategic Report. (2015). Retrieved February 12, 2017, from http://www.annualreport.g4s.com/pdfs/Strategic_report_G4S2015.pdf

33-9032 Security Guards. (2015, May). Retrieved February 12, 2017, from https://www.bls.gov/oes/current/oes339032.htm

49-2098 Security and Fire Alarm Systems Installers. (n.d.). Retrieved February 12, 2017, from https://www.bls.gov/oes/current/oes492098.htm

Brownyard, T. (2014, January 6). How Large Jury Settlements Affect Enterprise Security. Retrieved February 12, 2017, from http://www.securitymagazine.com/articles/85070-how-large-jury-settlements-affect-enterprise-security

CCTV and Video Surveillance Systems Market Trends. (n.d.). Retrieved February 12, 2017, from http://www.strategyr.com/MarketResearch/CCTV_Cameras_Video_Surveillance_Systems_Market_Trends.asp

Class "A" Private Investigative License, Class "B" Security Agency License, and Class "R" Recovery Agent License. (2014, February). Retrieved February 12, 2017, from http://forms.freshfromflorida.com/16022.pdf

Collins, P. A., Ricks, T. A., & Meter, C. W. (2015). *Principles of security and crime prevention*. Cincinnati, OH: Anderson Publishing Co.

FBI Releases Preliminary Semiannual Crime Statistics for 2016. (2017, January 09). Retrieved March 23, 2017, from https://www.fbi.gov/news/pressrel/press-releases/fbi-releases-preliminary-semiannual-crime-statistics-for-2016

Ford, R. H. (2011, February 25). NEGLIGENT SECURITY: WHEN IS CRIME YOUR PROBLEM? Retrieved February 12, 2017, from http://www.thefederation.org/documents/7.%20Negligent%20Security.pdf

Greenberg, D. F., & Roush, J. B. (2009, February). The Effectiveness of an Electronic Security Management System in a Privately Owned Apartment Complex. Retrieved February 12, 2017, from https://pdfs.semanticscholar.org/1987/179511f557eac03adc8dfe61c44afd04c54d.pdf

Griffin, J. (2013, September 30). ASIS 2014 educational session examines the Obamacare's impact on guard services providers. Retrieved February 12, 2017, from http://www.securityinfowatch.com/article/11707376/asis-2014-educational-session-examines-the-obamcares-impact-on-guard-services-providers

Jones, R. G. (2007, May 28). The Crime Rate Drops, and a City Credits Its Embrace of Surveillance Technology. Retrieved February 12, 2017, from http://www.nytimes.com/2007/05/29/nyregion/29east.html?ex=1182484800%40en&ei=5070

Markets and Markets › Summary: Video Surveillance Market worth 71.28 Billion USD by 2022. (2016). Retrieved February 12, 2017, from http://www.marketsandmarkets.com/PressReleases/global-video-surveillance-market.asp

Minnaar, A. (2012). PRIVATE SECURITY COMPANIES, NEIGHBOURHOOD WATCHES AND THE USE OF CCTV SURVEILLANCE IN RESIDENTIAL NEIGHBOURHOODS: THE CASE OF PRETORIA. Retrieved February 12, 2017, from https://www.researchgate.net/publication/275028522_PRIVATE_SECURITY_COMPANIES_NEIGHBOURHOOD_WATCHES_AND_THE_USE_OF_CCTV_SURVEILLANCE_IN_RESIDENTIAL_

NEIGHBOURHOODS_THE_CASE_OF_PRETORIA-EAST_ Anthony_Minnaar

Moody's Affirms U.S. Security's B3 CFR and Assigns Instrument Ratings to Proposed Refinancing; Outlook Stable. (2016, June 21). Retrieved February 12, 2017, from https://www.moodys.com/research/Moodys-Affirms-US-Securitys-B3-CFR-and-Assigns-Instrument-Ratings--PR_351019

Perry, R. H. (2016, July). White Paper on the U.S. Contract Security Industry. Retrieved February 12, 2017, from http://www.roberthperry.com/uploads/2016%20White%20Paper.pdf

Quick Facts: Resident Demographics. (n.d.). Retrieved February 12, 2017, from http://www.nmhc.org/Content.aspx?id=4708

Rice, D. (2015, February 9). State of the Market: Video Surveillance. Retrieved February 12, 2017, from http://www.sdmmag.com/articles/90911-state-of-the-market-video-surveillance

Richards, A., & Smith, H. (2007, January 1). Addressing the role of private security companies within security sector reform programmes. Retrieved February 2`, 2017, from https://www.files.ethz.ch/isn/39540/PSC_report.pdf

Securitas Annual Report 2015. (2016). Retrieved February 12, 2017, from http://ir.myreport.se/show/securitas/show.asp?pid=2354242510283&initPage

Sloan, V. (2007). The Constitution Project - Guidelines for Public Video Surveillance. *Guidelines for Public Video Surveillance*. Retrieved February 12, 2017, from http://www.constitutionproject.org/wp-content/uploads/2012/09/54.pdf

Staff, C. (n.d.). USC Campus Security: Taking It to the Streets. Retrieved February 12, 2017, from http://www.campussafetymagazine.com/article/USC-Campus-Security-Taking-It-to-the-Streets/P2

Storm, K., PhD. (2010, December). The Private Security Industry: A Review of the Definitions, Available Data Sources, and Paths Moving Forward. Retrieved February 12, 2017, from https://www.ncjrs.gov/pdffiles1/bjs/grants/232781.pdf

The effect of CCTV on public safety: Research roundup. (2017, February 09). Retrieved February 12, 2017, from https://journalistsresource.org/studies/government/criminal-justice/surveillance-cameras-and-crime

Vlahos, J. (2009, September 30). Surveillance Society: New High-Tech Cameras Are Watching You. Retrieved February 12, 2017, from http://www.popularmechanics.com/military/a2398/4236865/

www.ingramcontent.com/pod-product-compliance
Lightning Source LLC
Chambersburg PA
CBHW040248220526
45473CB00001B/412